United States Marine Corps

by Julie Murray

ABDO
U.S. ARMED FORCES
Kids

www.abdopublishing.com

Published by Abdo Kids, a division of ABDO, PO Box 398166, Minneapolis, Minnesota 55439.

Copyright © 2015 by Abdo Consulting Group, Inc. International copyrights reserved in all countries. No part of this book may be reproduced in any form without written permission from the publisher.

Printed in the United States of America, North Mankato, Minnesota.

052014

092014

Photo Credits: Alamy, AP Images, Getty Images, iStock, Shutterstock, Thinkstock, © Keith McIntyre / Shutterstock p.1, © User:diking / CC-BY-2.0 p.11

Production Contributors: Teddy Borth, Jennie Forsberg, Grace Hansen

Design Contributors: Candice Keimig, Laura Rask, Dorothy Toth

Library of Congress Control Number: 2013953956

Cataloging-in-Publication Data

Murray, Julie.

 United States Marine Corps / Julie Murray.

   p. cm. -- (U.S. Armed Forces)

ISBN 978-1-62970-096-0 (lib. bdg.) 4412304

Includes bibliographical references and index.

1. United States Marine Corps--Juvenile literature.   I. Title.

359.9--dc23

                2013953956

Table of Contents

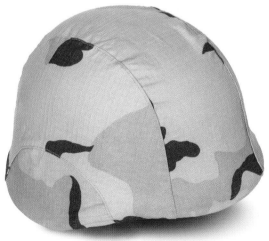

United States Marine Corps

The Marine Corps is a branch

of the U.S. **Armed Forces**.

The Marines keep the U.S. safe. They do this from the air, land, and sea.

The Marines help in **emergencies**. They help with floods and forest fires.

The Marines also guard

the White House.

11

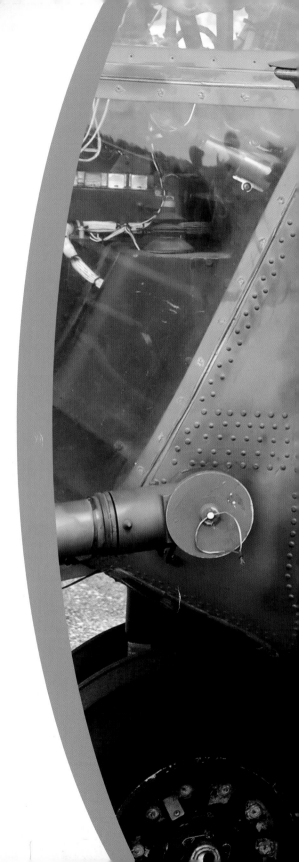

Jobs

There are many jobs

in the Marine Corps.

Mechanics fix things.

Pilots fly planes.

Cooks make food.

Vehicles and Weapons

The Marines use different kinds of **weapons**. They use fighter planes. The F/A-18 Hornet is a fighter plane.

They use **vehicles** that can go on land and water. They also use battle tanks. The M1 Abrams is a battle tank.

"Semper Fidelis"

The Marines keep Americans

safe every day!

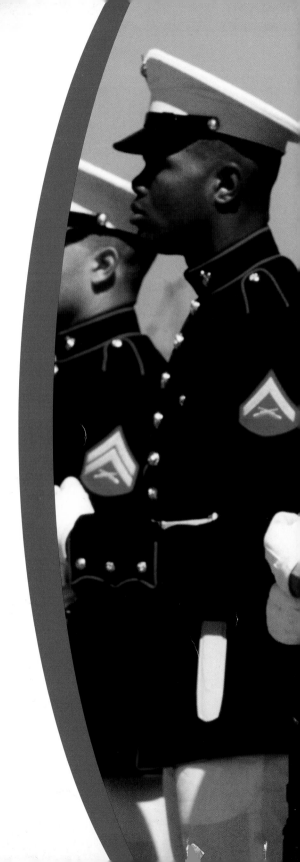

More Facts

- The English bulldog is the U.S. Marine Corps' mascot.

- The Marine Corps' motto is "Semper Fidelis." That is Latin for "Always faithful."

- The Marine Corps made Bugs Bunny an Honorary Master Sergeant after starring in the 1943 short film Super-Rabbit, where Bugs became a Marine.

Glossary

armed forces – military (land), naval (sea), and air forces (air). They protect and serve their nation.

emergency – a sudden event that requires help or relief.

vehicle – any means by which to travel. A car is a vehicle. Even a sled is a vehicle.

weapon – any object that is used in defense in combat.

Index

abdokids.com

Use this code to log on to abdokids.com and access crafts, games, videos and more!

Abdo Kids Code:
UUK0960